20 FUN FACTS ABOUT THE US FLAG

By Maria Nelson

Gareth Stevens
Publishing

Please visit our website, www.garethstevens.com. For a free color catalog of all our high-quality books, call toll free 1-800-542-2595 or fax 1-877-542-2596.

Library of Congress Cataloging-in-Publication Data

Nelson, Maria.
20 fun facts about the US flag / by Maria Nelson.
    p. cm. — (Fun fact file: US history)
Includes index.
ISBN 978-1-4339-9194-3 (pbk.)
ISBN 978-1-4339-9195-0 (6-pack)
ISBN 978-1-4339-9193-6 (library binding)
1. Flags—United States—Juvenile literature. I. Nelson, Maria. II. Title.
CR113.N46 2014
352.23—dc23

First Edition

Published in 2014 by
Gareth Stevens Publishing
111 East 14th Street, Suite 349
New York, NY 10003

Copyright © 2014 Gareth Stevens Publishing

Designer: Sarah Liddell
Editor: Greg Roza

Photo credits: Cover, p. 1 Amy Nichole Harris/Shutterstock.com; p. 5 XAOC/ Shutterstock.com; p. 6 Dorling Kindersley/Dorling Kindersley/Getty Images; p. 7 Kirsty Pargeter/Shutterstock.com; p. 8 Evelyn Peyton/E+/Getty Images; p. 9 Roel Smart/E+/ Getty Images; p. 10 Hulton Archive/Stringer/Hulton Archive/Getty Images; p. 11 photo courtesy of Wikimedia Commons, US Flag 15 stars.svg; p. 12 FPG/Staff/Archive Photos/ Getty Images; p. 13 Andersen Ross/Stockbyte/Getty Images; p. 14 (flag) photo courtesy of Wikimedia Commons, US Flag 48 stars.svg; p. 14 (Wilson) Stock Montage/Contributor/ Archive Photos/Getty Images; p. 15 C Flanigan/Contributor/FilmMagic/Getty Images; p. 16 Owen Franken/Photographer's Choice RF/Shutterstock.com; p. 18 Win McNamee/ Staff/Getty Images News/Getty Images; p. 19 Tetra Images/Getty Images; p. 20 Joe Fox/ Photographer's Choice RF/Getty Images; p. 21 Stocktrek Images/Getty Images; p. 22 Zigy Kaluzny/Stone/Getty Images; p. 23 photo courtesy of Wikimedia Commons, Major General Floyd L. Parks presented the Flag of Liberation to President Harry S. Truman in Berlin, Germany...-NARA-198680.jpg; p. 24 Kevin Clogstoun/Lonely Planet Images/Getty Images; p. 25 courtesy of Wikimedia Commons, Star Spangled Banner Flag on display at the Smithsonian's National Museum of History and Technology, around 1964.jpg; p. 26 Dieter Spears/E+/Getty Images; p. 27 Wash52121...Dan/Flickr Open/Getty Images; p. 29 (students) Dirk Anschutz/Stone/Getty Images; p. 29 (flag) lexaarts/Shutterstock.com.

Printed in the United States of America

CPSIA compliance information: Batch #CS13GS: For further information contact Gareth Stevens, New York, New York at 1-800-542-2595.

Contents

Words in the glossary appear in **bold** type the first time they are used in the text.

A National Symbol

The flag of the United States of America is known as a **symbol** of freedom around the world. Since the **American Revolution**, our nation has flown a banner of red, white, and blue. In fact, the modern **version** doesn't look that different from the first US flags.

Today, the US flag is a constant presence during both war and peacetime. The "Stars and Stripes" is flown on navy ships, in front of government buildings, and has even been to the moon!

How much do you know about the US flag? Read on to discover even more about the Stars and Stripes!

5

FACT 1

The first national flag had crosses on it, not stars.

As the 13 colonies fought for independence from Britain, they often flew the Continental Colors. This flag had 13 red-and-white stripes and a blue rectangle in the upper left-hand corner that featured a red cross and a white cross like a small British flag.

When the colonists officially broke from Britain during the war, stars replaced the crosses.

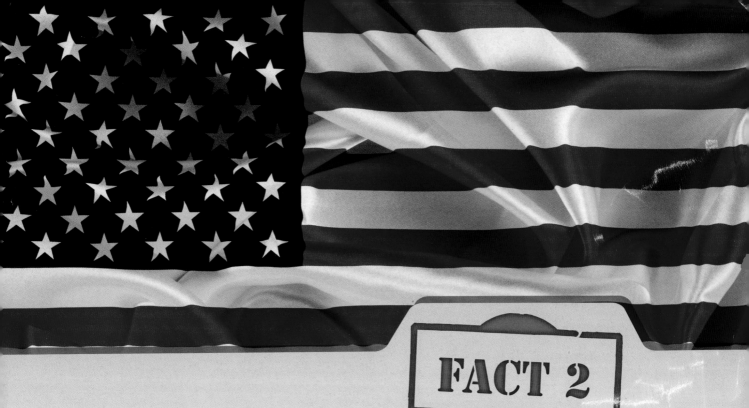

There are seven red stripes and six white stripes on the US flag.

The US flag's 13 stripes stand for the original 13 states in the union. Fifty stars symbolize the present 50 states. Some people think Puerto Rico may someday become the 51st state. If this happens, another star will be added to the flag.

Old Glory Red

White

Old Glory Blue

The US flag's official colors are White, Old Glory Red, and Old Glory Blue.

FACT 3

The exact shades of red, white, and blue to be used for all US flags were chosen in 1934.

The colors of the flag have been given meaning since they were first used on the Continental Colors flag. Red stands for bravery, white for purity and hope, and blue means justice and truth.

FACT 4

The first makers of the US flag used several different arrangements of stars.

The official flag was adopted in 1777. However, the arrangement for the stars wasn't clear. Some flag makers put the stars in rows, and some put them in a circle. The stars might have had five, six, or eight points!

In 1912, President Taft standardized both the arrangement of the stars on the flag and the flag's proportions. President Eisenhower slightly changed the stars' arrangement in 1959.

9

There's no recorded proof that Betsy Ross sewed the first US flag.

Betsy Ross's grandson said that in 1776, George Washington asked his grandmother to sew the US flag. However, this tale wasn't widely known until he told it in 1870. It's likely just a tall tale.

Between 1795 and 1818, the US flag had 15 stripes and 15 stars.

FACT 6

When a new state joins the union, a star is added to the flag on the following July 4.

At first, with the addition of a new state, both a star and a stripe were added to the flag. In 1818, a law passed that said only a star would be added. The stripes would always number 13.

FACT 7

The melody of "The Star-Spangled Banner" was taken from a British party song.

Francis Scott Key wrote the words to "The Star-Spangled Banner" in 1814. He had watched the flag fly over Fort McHenry as the British attacked it. The song became the official US national **anthem** in 1931.

Francis Scott Key

The Pledge of Allegiance was written in remembrance of the 400th anniversary of the discovery of America.

The Pledge of **Allegiance** was originally called the Youth's Companion Flag Pledge and was published in a Massachusetts magazine in 1892. The words have changed since then. The last time the words changed was in 1954.

National Flag Day falls on June 14. That's the date in 1777 when the first flag was approved.

President Woodrow Wilson chose the date of National Flag Day in 1916. Congress made June 14 an official day for honoring the flag in 1949. The president commonly declares a National Flag Week, too.

Woodrow Wilson

On Our Best Behavior

Only the president can change the federal rules about the flag.

The **Federal** Flag Code outlines how to act in the presence of the flag. It describes how the flag should be flown in special or unusual circumstances. It's not law, but it helps citizens show the flag respect.

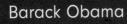
Barack Obama

A list of rules having to do with the flag was first compiled in 1923 at the National Flag Conference.

If the weather is bad, the flag shouldn't be flown.

The Federal Flag Code requires all government buildings to have a flagpole flying the US flag in front or nearby. In good weather, it's commonly flown from sunrise to sunset. When the flag is lit, it can be displayed 24 hours a day.

When Should the US Flag Be Flown?

The Flag Code states that the flag may be flown every day, but especially on some holidays, including these:

date	holiday
January 1	New Year's Day
February 12	President Abraham Lincoln's Birthday
third Sunday in May	Armed Forces Day
last Monday in May	Memorial Day
June 14	Flag Day
July 4	Independence Day
September 17	Constitution Day
November 11	Veterans Day
fourth Thursday in November	Thanksgiving Day

When a president or former president dies, the flag is flown at half-staff for 30 days.

Flying at half-staff means a flag is raised halfway up the flagpole. The US flag may fly at half-staff after a government official dies. A state's governor or the president can also call for this at other times.

The US flag shouldn't ever be used to cover a ceiling.

The Federal Flag Code gives very specific instructions on how the flag should be handled. It states that the flag should always be allowed to fly freely when displayed. Also, the flag shouldn't be folded or allowed to touch anything underneath it, such as the ground or floor.

It's legal to burn the US flag.

US flags too worn to be displayed may be disposed of by burning them in a respectful manner. The **Supreme Court** struck down the Flag Protection Act of 1989, which outlawed burning the flag. It said the law wouldn't have allowed freedom of expression.

Supporting the Armed Forces

FACT 15

When wearing a flag pin or patch, it should be fixed on the left side near the heart.

US military uniforms, as well as those of police officers and firefighters, have flag patches on them. The flag also flies from the masts of navy ships and is painted on the sides of fighter jets.

The US flag has long been used to show support for the US military as bumper stickers, pins, and small flags flown from houses around the nation.

FACT 16

The custom of draping a flag over a coffin during a military funeral started in Europe during the late 1700s.

When the US flag is removed from the coffin of a soldier who has passed away, it's folded 13 times in a special way and presented to family members. Each fold means something different. The first fold, for example, symbolizes life.

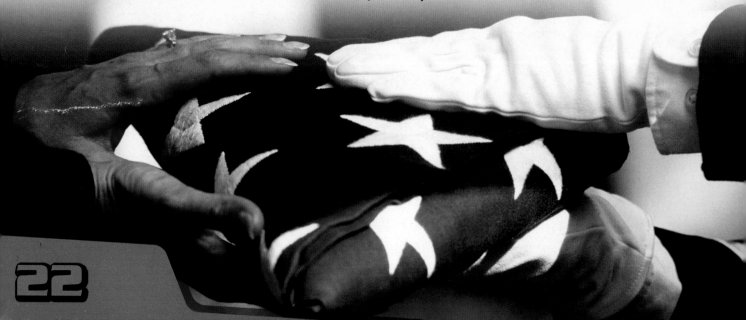

The "flag of liberation" was also flown when the United States declared war on Japan and a few days later when it declared war on Germany and Italy.

FACT 17

A flag was raised above the Capitol after Japan attacked Pearl Harbor in 1941 and drew the US into World War II.

President Franklin Roosevelt named it the "flag of **liberation**." He carried it with him several times. Many people think the same flag flew from the U.S.S. *Missouri* when Japan **surrendered** in 1945.

FACT 18

A high school student designed the modern US flag for a school project.

In 1958, 18-year-old Robert Heft earned a B minus on a **design** for the US flag with 50 stars. His teacher said if Congress accepted his design, he would get an A. He did!

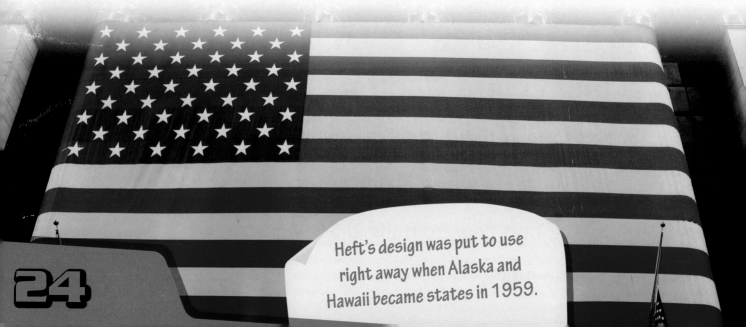

Heft's design was put to use right away when Alaska and Hawaii became states in 1959.

The "star-spangled banner" that Francis Scott Key wrote about is still around—and you can see it!

Lieutenant Colonel George Armistead commanded Fort McHenry in 1814. He kept the flag that flew above the battle! Today, it's on display at the National Museum of American History in Washington, DC.

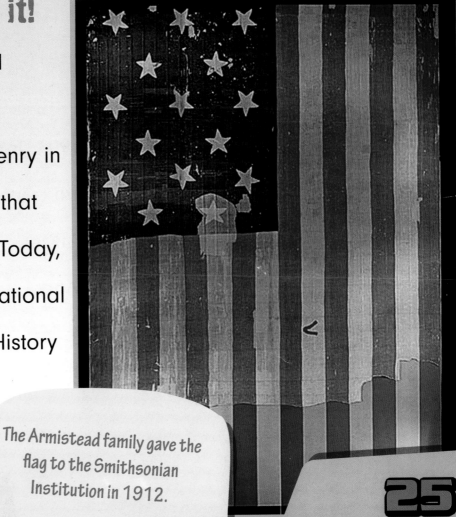

The Armistead family gave the flag to the Smithsonian Institution in 1912.

FACT 20

A person who studies flags is called a vexillologist.

A team has been working to preserve the "star-spangled banner" since 1994. In order to do this, they've had to learn a lot about the flag. Vexillologists' specialized knowledge can help those **preserving** flags to stay true to a flag's time period and history.

The US Flag Through the Years

1989
The Supreme Court strikes down a law against flag burning, saying it's a form of free speech.

1949
Congress declares June 14 National Flag Day.

1818
It's established that the star for each new state would be added to the flag on the following July 4.

1777
The Flag Act states that the US flag will have 13 white stars on a field of blue and 13 stripes, alternating between white and red.

1960
A flag with 50 stars is adopted.

1912
President Howard Taft issues an order that lists the flag's proportions and the first official arrangement of stars.

1814
Francis Scott Key writes the words to "The Star-Spangled Banner."

Flying with Pride

Whether called "Old Glory" or just the Stars and Stripes, the US flag has **represented** our nation for more than 200 years. We remove our caps when the national anthem is sung and place our hands over our hearts. Songs such as "You're a Grand Old Flag" have remained common in schools around the country.

When you see a flag, remember how closely it's tied to the moments that have won America's freedom. And salute our star-spangled banner as it flies in the breeze!

US children start the school day by reciting the Pledge of Allegiance in front of the US flag.

29

Glossary

allegiance: loyalty to one's country or leader

American Revolution: the war in which the colonies won their freedom from England

anthem: a song declaring loyalty to a group, cause, or country

design: the pattern or shape of something. Also, to create the pattern or shape of something.

federal: having to do with the national government

liberation: the act of setting free

preserve: to keep something in its original state

represent: to stand for

Supreme Court: the highest court in the United States

surrender: to give up

symbol: a picture or shape that stands for something else

version: a form of something that is different from the ones that came before it

For More Information

Books

Allen, Kathy. *The First American Flag*. Minneapolis, MN: Picture Window Books, 2010.

Eldridge, Alison, and Stephen Eldridge. *The American Flag: An American Symbol*. Berkeley Heights, NJ: Enslow Elementary, 2012.

White, Becky. *Betsy Ross*. New York, NY: Holiday House, 2011.

Websites

Ben's Guide: Symbols of US Government

bensguide.gpo.gov/3-5/symbols/index.html

Learn fun facts about the American flag as well as other symbols and important places in US history.

USA for Kids: The Flag

www.usconsulate.org.hk/pas/kids/sym_flag.htm

Read more about the history of the US flag, and use links to learn interesting information about the United States.

Index